D1241247

PHENOMENOLOGY
AND HUMANISM

PHENOMENOLOGY
AND HUMANISM

A PRIMER IN EXISTENTIAL PHENOMENOLOGY

William A. Luijpen

DUQUESNE UNIVERSITY PRESS, PITTSBURGH, PA.
Editions E. Nauwelaerts, Louvain

By William A. Luijpen
Existential Phenomenology, 5th impression
Phenomenology and Atheism
Phenomenology and Metaphysics
Phenomenology of the Natural Law

Library of Congress Catalog Card Number 66–28339

All rights reserved

© 1966 by Duquesne University

Printed in the U.S.A.

CONTENTS

v

PHENOMENOLOGICAL
REDUCTION AND THE
"LIVED-WORLD"

1

Merleau-Ponty once wrote that phenomenology meant "the disavowal of science." What difficulties phenomenology has had to face because of this sentence! How much trouble the phenomenologists could have spared themselves had they expressed themselves more clearly about their relationship to the sciences. If phenomenology really were the disavowal of science, what else then could it be but mystification of reality? And how was the reader of that or similar sentences to know that he was not dealing with a new and persistent form of philosophical mysticism? Most of the objections to phenomenology seem to take the form of an accusation of mysticism. This does not mean, however, that all will be well with phenomenology once the charge of mysticism is removed. A deeper understanding of phenomenological thought leads inexorably to a confrontation with the very questions and answers which have preoccupied man since the dawn of civilization.

We want to concern ourselves here, however, with the difficulties arising out of a first and necessarily limited philosophical contact with phenomenology. Much of the blame for the confusion in the mind of the reader must be placed at the feet of the phenomenologists.

Any scientist, in whatever type of scientific endeavor, seeks to express the objective meaning of reality. There are phenomenologists, however, who resist any claim to objectivity. How then shall we blame the scientists when they accuse phenomenology of subjectivism? Any real scientific insight is often seen as absolute. The phenomenologist obviously feels repelled by any claim to "absolute knowledge." Yet, is it not inevitable that this position forces him to defend himself against relativism?

The scientists see their efforts both as true accomplishments and as real fulfilments of human reason. There are, however, phenomenologists who do not want to hear of rational knowledge. But does this not imply that phenomenology is really only one of the many forms of irrationalism? Some phenomenologists do not attach any importance to the idea of essence and the correlate, objective universality of philosophy, especially in so far as it concerns the essence of man. What else can such disregard imply but the abandonment of the ideal of philosophy as SCIENTIA SCIENTIARUM? And does not this position necessarily lead to a radical situation ethics?

If finally we note how some phenomenologists seem to deny the subjective universality of truth, we ask ourselves whether phenomenology can yield anything but interesting diaries or entertaining novels with philosophical implications. But how can a real philosopher follow in all earnestness a train of thought which at the outset is defined as "the disavowal of science"?

We can understand and appreciate this radical utterance only after we investigate what the scientists have done to such concepts as "scientific," "objective," "absolute," and "rational." We then will discover the many hidden and unwarranted assumptions and presuppositions which were smuggled inside the legitimate confines of these concepts. In fact, scientific disciplines often degenerated into a *scientism*. The "disavowal of the sciences" by Merleau-Ponty therefore does not imply a criticism of the results of the sciences, it does not seek to question the validity of physical laws or the veracity of mathematical equations, but rather seeks to break the dictatorship and absolutism of scientific thought over all other forms of human thinking.

The Absolutism of the Sciences: A Contradiction

When science had degenerated into scientism, we were asked to believe that there would be only one way to talk objectively about reality and this way was exemplified by the physicist. We were asked to believe that the only objective real world would be the one the physicist talks about. We were asked to believe that there would be only one way to experience reality and this way was exemplified by the experimental method of the physicist. We had to accept the fact that our spontaneous and ordinary experience of the world would have to be replaced by a system of scientific experiences. The physicist would be the one to teach us the meaning of the real world. Phenomenology represents a revolt against these impossible demands, impossible because they include a fundamental contradiction. *Phenomenology is the disavowal of scientism.*

In what does the contradiction of scientism consist and how does phenomenology make this contradiction visible? Already before the era of phenomenology many philosophers had pointed out that the one who adheres to scientism in his act of rejecting philosophy, becomes, in fact, a philosopher himself. His talk about scientific methodology and objective truth contains an implicit, and in principle complete, epistemology as well as a philosophy of reality.

The phenomenologist adds to this the observation that we never could become aware of the real world if we accept the premise that only the physicist is capable of expressing the objective meaning of the world. In that way of thinking, only scientific experience can bring us into contact with the objective world; our spontaneous, ordinary every-day experiences would be powerless in that regard.

This constitutes a contradiction: not a contradiction in terms, but a contradiction with "life," with the life of the scientist himself.

A Few Examples

How is it that I learn the meaning of landscapes, rivers and seas? Is it really through books on geography that I gain this meaning? Whoever proposes such a solution fools himself. It is true that a book on geography contains worthwhile scientific knowledge pertaining to landscapes, seas and rivers, but this knowledge is accessible to me only on the basis of a more fundamental and absolutely original experience; this experience comprises our every day spontaneous contact with landscapes, seas and rivers.

The geographer himself would not really know about what he is writing, if he would *not* accept the fact that he treats of mountains and valleys which he knew *before* he ever knew the meaning of the word geography (Merleau-Ponty).

What is a boy to do if he wants to get to know a girl? Should he consult some treatise on human physiology? He had better be advised to invite the girl to his birthday party. If the books on physiology and anatomy do not concern themselves with girls who can be experienced as real on a festive occasion, or in the classroom or on the streetcar, then these books treat of nothing. As soon as we deny for a moment the reality of our ordinary daily experience of girls, we lose the coherence and meaning of any treatise on female physiology and anatomy. A scientific treatise only makes sense so long as it is seen against the background of our ordinary everyday experience of whatever the treatise is dealing with. How surprising then, that people, who want to give sexual information to children, prepare themselves for this task so often with readings in physiology and anatomy!

The spontaneous, everyday experience teaches me that I live in a world in which apples fall down from a tree and not sideways or upward (De Waelhens), in which the sun rises and sets (Merleau-Ponty). The physicist came up with the idea that the sun remains stationary, or nearly so, and we were immediately ready to call our own experience of our own lived-world (*Lebenswelt*) an illusion. But what kind of a world has the physicist in mind if it is not the world over which the sun rises and sets? Sometimes a physicist has overworked and has damaged his health or his mental balance. His physician then tells him to stay out of the world of the stationary sun for a while and to seek some rest in the one with sunrises and sunsets. Then the miracle occurs—the physicist regains his health and his mental balance in a world which he had refused to call objective.

The Lived-World As Our Objective World

What is the true object of the sciences? With what do the sciences really occupy themselves? To gain insight into these questions we need to restore the lived-world to a position of prominence in our thinking. As a first step toward this restoration we must acknowledge the objectivity of this lived-world. This step implies the renunciation of the claim that only the sciences can speak about a real world; that only scientific thought merits the label of objective validity.

The history of philosophy shows us how scientific experience gradually took the place of our spontaneous everyday experience of the world; the objects of the sciences replaced the ensemble of meanings of our lived-world. It is largely in Descartes' thought that the lived-world was destroyed in its spontaneous immediacy. The only legitimate, objective approach to the real world becomes here one of quantification. Only the clearly delineated concepts of quantity are judged adequate to describe the world. His methodological use of doubt is but a means for achieving a privileged status for scientific knowledge. This essentially constitutes the philosophy of *scientism*.

Disregard of Knowledge As Immediate Presence

The theory of primary and secondary qualities contains an implicit theory of experience and of knowledge. The primary qualities are acknowledged as objective, the secondary qualities as merely subjective. But in the *initial experience* of an apple, for example, the distinction between size (primary quality) and color (secondary quality) fails to appear. Both aspects actually appear to us and both appear as equally real. Yet, the quantitative aspect, the readily measurable aspect of the apple, is accorded a primacy, is designated as objective. What is the true meaning of this discrimination between two aspects of an object? This discrimination actually amounts to an interpretation of knowledge and experience in which the immediate presence of reality is devaluated. The priority of the quantitative aspect of the apple over its color certainly is not given in our immediate presence to that apple. As soon as immediate experience of present reality is devaluated, as soon as the dialogue between immediate presence (man) and present reality (world) is interrupted, we have an epistemology in which knowledge is considered as a *mirror reflection* and the world as a *world-in-itself*.

"Back to the Things Themselves"

Up to now we have considered the two erroneous postulates which have dominated Western philosophy since Descartes. Knowledge was seen as a mirroring of reality, as a reflecting representation of a *world-in-itself*, and *the* system of objective re-presentation par excellence is that of the physical sciences (De Waelhens). These two postulates violate reality as it actually appears in our immediate presence. All phenomenologists are united in their struggle against these misconceptions and they demand that we accept reality as it appears immediately in our experience and without the sub-terfuge of all kinds of theoretical pre-judgments. The Husserlian phrase "back to the things themselves" formulates in a nutshell this intention to return to the world of original experience and the wealth of meanings which can be found there. This return must be made without any prior theorizing about experience and without *a priori* elimination of any realms of meaning whatsoever.

Scientism seeks to *replace* our spontane-ous everyday experience with scientific experience; it also seeks to *replace* the *lived-world* with objects of the natural sciences. It is precisely here that the con-tradiction of scientism emerges. We can-not eliminate this contradiction even if we are ready to accept the primacy of our spontaneous everyday experience but yet try to view this experience in the manner which is customary in empirical psychol-ogy. The numerous treatises on condi-tioning, neural reflexes, excitation potentials, etc., nevertheless fail to express our experience as it originally emerges. Our original experience certainly does not consist of a conglomeration of concepts, views and laws of the different branches of natural science. The opposite is true: the different sciences *presuppose* original everyday experience and without this presupposition nobody would ever know what "conditioning" or "neural reflexes" could possibly refer to. Reflexes, excitation potentials, conditioning schemata all point to the world of our ordinary, everyday experiences. To think that these scientific conceptualizations could *replace* this world is preposterous and contradictory, precisely because these conceptualizations depend upon this world in order to have any meaning at all.

The Phenomenological Reduction

The concept of phenomenological reduction constantly recurs in the work of Husserl. The final formulation of this in chologism he read Brentano, one of the very few anti-psychologismic thinkers of that era. Here he became acquainted with the concept of intentionality, which, contrary to Brentano's teaching, he came to regard as the essence of knowledge and consciousness. To get to know something, to be conscious of something, essentially means to find ourselves intending, to find ourselves directed toward some reality which is not consciousness nor knowledge itself. To be conscious means to be beyond this consciousness on the way to some reality which is not this consciousness itself. And it is the presence of this intended reality which ultimately decides questions of truth and certitude.

The first form of reduction which we find mentioned in Husserl's writing is that of "placing between brackets" the factual existence of the things which are presented in consciousness. What prompted Husserl to this temporary suspension of all judgments concerning the factual existence of appearing reality? To understand this we must remember the predominance of the critical problem in the philosophies of the nineteenth century. This critical problem asks about the existence of a reality which would actually correspond to the representations received by an isolated, closed *Cogito*. In order to by-pass the quicksand of these discussions, Husserl introduced the concept of bracketing. The fact that Husserl places between brackets the concerns regarding the actual existence of what appears real to us, the fact that he suspends ultimate reality judgments, the fact that he refuses to commit himself to an assessment of the ontological status of things, all clearly indicate the extent to which Husserl himself was still the victim of the very *Cogito* myths which he fought so hard to dispel (De Waelhens).

Only within a philosophical framework in which the *Cogito* is seen as isolated and encapsuled can there be place for doubt concerning the factual existence of things. Husserl failed to see at that time that the concept of intentionality as he had originally formulated it precluded the possibility of a phenomenological reduction designed to bracket the factual existence of the objects of our world.

If consciousness truly is intentionality then no question can possibly arise concerning the reality of the world intended in this consciousness; rather we should say that without the factually existing world, consciousness could not be what it is, namely intentionality. In Husserl's work there is a gradual development in which less and less value is attached to this bracketing procedure, but the value of the phenomenological reduction is stressed more and more. This trend implies a development in which the reduction acquires a new meaning. Husserl does not deviate from his original intentions for phenomenology; he continues to see phenomenology as a method that will lead us to the indisputable by way of a return to the *things themselves*.

It is the things themselves which are

immediately accessible in our experience. Husserl understood, however, that the then current notions of experience ran contrary to his own conceptions. In Husserl's conception, experience is presence to the things themselves. Only when experience is viewed in this way can it serve as a foundation upon which all true statements can securely rest. The popular notions of experience as Husserl found them at the turn of the century were severely distorted conceptualizations which were made to order to fit in a so-called scientific view of man and world. The phenomenological reduction therefore can ultimately be viewed as an instrument by means of which we can filter out the distorting influences of cultural and scientific prejudices.

The evolution of Husserl's thinking in this respect has been an exceedingly complicated one and the final term of that evolution is by no means entirely clear. It is Merleau-Ponty who has clarified these final stages of Husserl's thought.

Phenomenology when seen as an endeavor to uncover the foundations of philosophy, when seen as a method by means of which we can reach the indisputable ground of truth, needs to unmask all philosophical prejudices concerning the nature of consciousness. This unmasking brings in its wake the reinstatement of actual experience as it is lived, namely, as presence to and uncovering of the *lived-world*.

CONSCIOUSNESS AS
INTENTIONALITY

ished and ready in a world-in-itself.
Idealism finds its source of meaning in
the isolated *Cogito*. Knowledge is here
but an immanent development of meaning.

Prehistory of the Concept of Inten-tionality

Intentionality, *in Husserl's view*, implies
irrevocably the denial of both idealism
and realism. This is not true of the concept of intentionality as it was developed
by Brentano, or of the same thought as
it appeared before in scholasticism. Scholastic philosophy offers a view in which
consciousness is separated from the sur-
rounding and contrasting reality *first*,
only *subsequently* to be brought into contact with reality by means of a *forma
vicaria*. This vicarious form, this imprinted image, is but a delegate of and a
replacement for the real, brute reality.
When we raise the question of being in
connection with these forms, scholasticism will answer that these do not pos-

sess an "entitative being" (*esse entitativum*) but an "intentional being" (*esse intentionale*). This latter expression indicates that the being of these forms consist wholly in their referring to reality. Yet, it is clear that the whole necessity for postulating these "vicarious forms" stems from the original separation of *Cogito* and world-in-itself. If consciousness is seen as a being present to reality, as a being involved and a being caught up in reality, we clearly have no need for certain "vicarious forms" to effect contact between consciousness and world.

Husserl's Conception

In Husserl's thinking consciousness *itself* is intentional. Consciousness is seen as presence to a reality which this conness itself is not. This presence and accessibility to reality is not seen as a subsequent elaboration of a pre-existing, originally isolated consciousness; consciousness *is* this accessibility to reality. The Cartesian method of doubt proceeds

27

by cutting the *Cogito* loose from the world, only to subsequently reintegrate this world insides the confines of the *Cogito* itself, be it with the indicator "thought of" (*pensée de*, Merleau-Ponty). Trees, houses and chairs now become *thoughts* of trees, houses and chairs. Phenomenology refuses this *Cogito* as an "illusion of immanence" (Sartre). The essence of consciousness is precisely this open movement toward an accessible reality which this *consciousness itself* is *not*. To question the reality of the world is absurd in this context. The reality of the world is the guarantor of the *Cogito*. The true scandal of philosophy is not its failure to provide absolute proof for the factual existence of the world (Kant) but rather its persistence in asking for this absurd proof (Heidegger).

Nor can phenomenology acquiesce in a realism which starts from a world-in-itself, from a reality which, while outside the true confines of the *Cogito*, awaits the accurate mirror reflection by a passive consciousness. Husserl's philosophy of intentionality overcomes realism in so far as it poses consciousness as already actively involved in the world. This active consciousness allows the world to be what it is. It is impossible to think of the world in the absence of human consciousness because thinking itself is intentionality, i.e., a mode of being involved in the world. To consider the world in the absence of human consciousness would mean to withdraw from the very object which we seek to penetrate. No real question can be asked under such circumstances.

The Objectivity of the World

At this point the question of the objectivity of the world arises in the mind of many readers. But might not this question arise precisely because the reader seeks an objective reality which lies outside the realm of consciousness? Is it not because he still wants to think of the world as separated from the realm of thought? One thing is sure: the objectivity of the world should not be interpreted in an objectivistic manner. Objective reality cannot be thought about if such reality is considered to be prior to thought, and therefore prior to consciousness. Our very thinking of an objective reality always *already* involves us in that reality and precludes any "knowledge" prior to that involvement. The term "objective reality" cannot possibly apply to a reality considered in the absence of consciousness. A world considered in the absence of consciousness is a *non-sensical* world. All real knowledge of such a world becomes an impossibility, since real knowledge implies conscious involvement in a world.

But neither should we interpret the objectivity of the world in a subjectivistic manner. We cannot say just anything that comes up in our mind and still claim to speak objectively concerning a reality. Objectivity is the *alētheia*, the unconcealedness of the things them-

selves. The things are drawn from con-
cealedness by the activity of consciousness, by its "letting be" of reality (*seinlassen*). Consciousness is not merely
passive (as in realism) but rather is the
active revelation of objects. Without
this active revelation of consciousness
man is without any world whatsoever.
The intellect is an *intellectus agens* (Scholasticism). Yet, neither is consciousness
pure activity (as in idealism); it is sensi-
tive to and receptive toward the things
themselves as they break through to consciousness with a certain urgency. The
intellect also is *intellectus patiens* (Scholasticism).

To summarize and unify these two
aspects, we describe consciousness as *encounter*. It now becomes clear why the
phenomenologist objects to all pretenses
of objectivity and ultimacy of knowledge. The phenomenologist objects to
the objectivistic and absolutistic interpretation of truth. Truth is not a question
of correspondence between our knowl-

edge and a meaning which belongs to a world separated from human consciousness. With this in mind we can speak without qualms concerning the "subjectivity" of all truth if we understand this to mean that all knowledge expresses objectivity as it appears to a *subject*. Furthermore, we can reinterpret the statement that "all truth is relative" to mean that all truth expresses a relationship to a subject: in its *relationship* to a subject truth is absolute.

It is now clear why the "so-called critical problem" in its traditional form ceases to be a problem if intentionality is seen as a being-directed-toward-the-world, as a unity of mutual implication of world and consciousness (Kwant). The "critical problem" itself cannot form the basis for a rejection of the concept of intentionality. If the critical problem exists, then it must be expressed in terms derived from knowledge as it actually exists and not by means of an *a priori* philosophy of the *Cogito* (Heidegger).

has followed our argument with interest and may be even with approval, may now shake their heads in disbelief when he reads the preceding paragraph. He might even doubt the sanity of the phenomenologist who wrote it first. Nevertheless, it is Heidegger who in full possession of his faculties wrote that: *"wenn kein Dasein existiert ist keine Welt da"*; "without *Dasein* there is no world." This statement, strange as it may appear at first sight, nevertheless draws a careful and ultimate conclusion from the concept of intentionality. Nobody can with truth call himself a phenomenologist if he does not subscribe wholly to this basic thought. To reject it is to automatically bring us back to Cartesianism. Actually, the thought here expressed by Heidegger is highly accessible, if we realize that the phenomenological "return to the things themselves" implies at the same time a return to the "speaking word" (*parole parlante*, Merleau-Ponty). This "speaking word" is the living word; it is the only word that *really speaks*. This word implies a subject who makes use of the "spoken word" (*parole parlée*) to express reality. Whoever makes use of the word *being* in the sense of a speaking word intends to affirm a particular reality. If we use the verb "to be" in any of its forms and if we do not intend to affirm anything with it we are not really saying anything at all. The verb "to be" has meaning only when a subject seeks to affirm a reality which exists for that subject. "To be" implies man, for whom things are! Heidegger says nothing strange when he states that "without *Dasein* there can be no world"; without man there *is* nothing, since being always means being-for-man. Being is always and necessarily a "what" and a "how"; it is a meaning which cannot be separated from the *Cogito*. "Being and truth are convertible" (*ens et verum convertuntur*, Scholasticism).

Objections

The preceding argument is often criticized on the basis that *in knowledge itself* the world is revealed as *independent* of my consciousness. It is argued that phenomenology denies this when it makes the world dependent on consciousness, when it states that there is no world without man. This argument is based on a misunderstanding. Although it is true that the world reveals itself in knowledge as independent of consciousness, we should not therefore conclude that it would be possible to affirm this world outside the realm of human affirmation, i.e., outside the realm of knowledge and consciousness. Only in this affirmation does the verb "to be" acquire its meaning. The fact that the world appears in knowledge as independent from consciousness means no more than that consciousness cannot be the efficient cause of the world. *Man as intentional being is himself the affirmer-of-the-world;* this aspect forms part of the essence of man. Man cannot ignore or go beyond his own essence.

This same line of reasoning requires us to state that without man there can be no God (for man). This is not atheism.

"If there is a God, He must be a God-for-me" (Jolivet). Sartre is not an atheist because he feels that he cannot affirm something that lies outside his realm of possible affirmation. Nor is Marcel a theist because he feels that this affirmation is possible. It is not the task of metaphysics to imagine beings which cannot be thought.

Here we often meet with the objection that phenomenology represents really nothing new. This must be fully admitted: phenomenology is not something drastically novel. It is not the intention of the phenomenologist to unlock doors that are already open. He merely seeks to point to the already open doors and thus invite people to enter through them (Rümke).

Sartre Is Not a Phenomenologist But a Cartesian Thinker

Sartre gives extensive descriptions of the world-in-itself (*monde-en-soi*). These descriptions are pure nonsense, yet, with a

little effort we can at least learn about
the source of this nonsense. Sartre describes the "in-itself" in terms of compact
density, complete positivity, as filled up
entirely with itself, etc. The "in-itself"
is fully what it is, fully identical with itself, maintaining no relations with what
it is not, including no negations whatsoever, so that, when it disappears we are
not even able to say that it is no longer.
The "in-itself" cannot be derived from
the possible, nor can it be based on the
necessary. It is not created and it has no
reason for being; it simply *is*, hanging as
it were in the midst of nowhere.

The informed reader can easily see that
this so-called description of the "in-
itself" stands in the service of the descrip
tion of the "in-itself-for-him" (*en-soi-
pour lui*). Sartre sees very well that the
"in-itself-for-him" maintains relations,
that it is not full positivity, that it is no
longer when it disappears, etc. He turns
all the qualifications of the "in-itself-
for-him" around and hopes that this list

will describe the "in-itself." The "in-itself" is not the "for-him." All the qualifications of the "in-itself-for-him" define the "in-itself" with the help of a negative sign. Sartre artificially suspends the intentional movement of the "for itself" and yet insists that he is speaking meaningfully. "At this moment the word absurdity flows from my pen" (*Nausea*). Sartre notes himself that the "in-itself" is absurd! But it is not the "in-itself" which is absurd, it is absurd to want to speak about an "in-itself"! Sartre stops being a phenomenologist the moment he starts to describe the "in-itself." And *absolutized "in-itself"* brings in its wake an absolutized "for-itself." Since the "for-itself" is described as freedom we may expect that this freedom will also be absolutized. This is indeed the case. But this absolutizing leads to a further denial of intentionality.

MAN AS EXISTENCE

Existentialism and Phenomenology

Heidegger's thought does not simply continue along the path indicated by his mentor Husserl. Something distinctly new is added and this new element is derived from Kierkegaard. Heidegger's thought represents a fusion, as it were, of two related but separate streams of thought. This fusion generally goes by the name of existential phenomenology. Kierkegaard sees man as existence, as movement of the subject toward that which the subject is not himself, as a movement toward God. There is a distinct similarity between this description of man and Husserl's description of intentionality. Existentialism in Kierkegaard's terms implies a radical expression of the absolutely concrete, radically subjective and completely original, unrepeatable individuality. This view is incompatible with all striving toward subjective and objective universalities. Existentialism derives from this its early anti-scientific bias. In this view, philosophical knowledge could claim to be philosophical only in so far as it renounced all pretenses of being scientific knowledge, i.e., of being universally valid in the objective as well as in the subjective sense.

Husserl, however, sought a philosophy as a "rigorous science," as characterized by universal subjective and objective validity. Objective validity could be reached through the "vision of essence" (*Wesenschau*) of objects which resulted from the eidetic reduction. In this latter reduction the phenomenologist suspends the particularity of a contemplated reality in order to reach its essence. With the aid of the method of free variation Husserl attempted to separate the essence of a reality from its peripheral aspects. This recovery of the essence introduced the objective and universally valid moment in the act of knowing and Husserl therefore could rightfully speak of a phenomenological *science*.

In Heidegger we find a *scientific* ontology of man as openness. This ontology has been achieved through a phenomenology enriched with a variety of themes derived from existentialism. With the aid of a *scientifically* valid phenomenological method Heidegger is trying to realize a general, scientifically valid theory of man as existence, of man as openness. Existentialism and phenomenology thus flow together and form a new unity. In this unity existentialism provides the themes which, with the help of phenomenology, deepen into a valid ontology of man. The fact that this labor was undertaken by Heidegger resulted in a "detheologizing" of Kierkegaard's thought.

The Intractability of Jaspers and Marcel

The anti-scientific bias of existentialism continues in the thought of Jaspers and Marcel. This thinking is in constant contradiction to itself in so far as it im-

plicitly seeks to be more than a mere
monologue. To take the anti-scientific
position of Jaspers and Marcel literally
would mean that the thought of an
existentialist would lose validity in all
situations except his own. But what then
can be the point of communicating this
thought to *us?* Does not this communica-
tion imply the presence of general patterns which apply to *us?* The overt denial
of common patterns which bind individ-
uals together no doubt contributes its
share to the present decline in importance of these two thinkers. This is not
to deny that both Jaspers and Marcel
contribute some fascinating pages to the
history of philosophy, especially when
they react against the *absolute knowledge*
of idealism or against notions concerning
the intersubjective character proper to
truth in science, in the narrow sense of
this term.

The statement that philosophical truth
cannot be generally valid in a subjective
and objective sense is itself contradictory

because a philosophical statement acquires meaning only after subjective and objective generalities are *presupposed*. Husserl saw this clearly. Jaspers and Marcel did not undergo the influence of phenomenology and it is this fact in particular that must be considered in the evaluation of the decline in importance of these thinkers. This decline is all the more regrettable since these thinkers maintained the original religious inspiration of Kierkegaard. This (probably) is not the case in Heidegger's work.

Between Materialistic and Spiritualistic Monism

Phenomenology in its development toward an ontology of man has opened to our view a midway between materialistic monism and spiritualistic monism (Dondeyne). All materialistic systems of thought agree in one respect: man is seen as the end result of cosmic processes and forces, a thing amidst other things, a plateau or rest point in the endless evolution of the cosmos. It should be clear that such a strong and historically deeply rooted philosophy as materialism cannot be simply ignored or be thought of as speaking of nothing real. Yet, the materialistic philosopher forever finds it difficult to explain his own existence with the aid of concepts used to explain the existence of objects. This difficulty is due in part to the fact that "things" do not develop philosophies, not even materialistic ones! Materialism always by-passes human subjectivity. As a philosophy it amounts to a form of "detotalization of reality" (Le Senne).

This weak point in the materialist's argument furnishes his opponents with a totally new point of departure. Every spiritualist sees the necessity for according a certain primacy to subjectivity. If really nothing existed outside objects, this fact could not even be stated. We only can make this statement because man is a subject and not a thing. The *Cogito* indeed is undeniable (Descartes).

49

Spiritualistic monism, however, exaggerates the meaning of the subject; it tends to enlarge the importance of the subject till it assumes absolute autonomy and acquires the status of a godlike Ego. Against the backdrop of this gigantic ego, the objects of the world lose their density; they evaporate into mere contents of consciousness. Existential philosophy has clearly recognized both the strong and the weak features of materialistic and spiritualistic monism. Man therefore is not defined as *thing*, nor as absolute ego, but as existence, as being-conscious-in-the-world, as unity of mutual implication of subjectivity and world (Kwant).

Pointing out and Proving

The claim that being-man should be defined as existence, as being-conscious in the world, cannot be proven in a strictly logical sense. Defining man this way becomes legitimate only on the basis of an insight which is irreducible to

a more general insight. A philosopher
can merely "point" to this definition.
This surely is an unfortunate matter, yet,
there is no escape from it. We all must
start by pointing to an intended reality;
without this we shall never know about
what we speak. Speaking is already a
"bringing to view and to light" of a
reality. If speaking fails to do this we
have mere empty sound. The philosopher
speaks and this speaking brings to view
that which he has seen. Husserl said "it
is impossible to reach agreement with a
person who either cannot or does not
want to see."

There are several ways in which we
can show that being-human means existence. As a point of departure we might
take the meaning of the human body.
Whoever wants to express in words the
meaning of the human body does well to
work through and beyond the Cartesian
conceptions. Here, the body is seen as *a*
body as belonging to "the large family
of bodies." To conceive of the human

body merely as *a* body is to by-pass the very essence of the object of our research; it means that we overlook the fact that we deal with a *human* body, i.e., the body-of-a-subject. The human body is always "my body," or "yours," or "his." Biology and physiology cannot tell us what the *human* body is and anatomy cannot draw it for us. The *human* body does not appear in biology, anatomy or physiology books. The body which is described there is not *my* body, *your* body, *his* or *her* body. Instead it is *a* body and as such belongs to the world of objects. But the human body does not belong to the objects in the world; it belongs on the side of the subject (Dondeyne).

This formulation does justice to my bodily experience. The hands with which I grasp things are not themselves objects to be grasped; these hands are I-myself-grasping-things. My feet are not themselves part of the world-to-be-walked-on; whoever walks on my feet will meet with

world accessible and why is it accessible
in this way and not in another? We must
look to our feet for at least part of the
answers. If I had webbed feet or wings,
the world would present itself as accessible in different ways. Why is there a
audible world and a visible world? Part
of the answer again must bring us back to
our body; to our ears and eyes. If I had
the eyes of a rat or of an owl, the perspective of the world would drastically
change. I am an incarnated subject and
the world sticks to this incarnated subject as a system of meanings. Sirius is
"far away" because I cannot grasp it;
the Rocky Mountains are high because
I cannot tower over them; the sidewalk
is low because I can step on it from the
mainroad without trouble. Why is the
world hard, soft, cold, warm, angular,
sticky, resistant or immobile? The world
shows all these meanings in its relationship to the incarnated subject, which I
am. In fact we have explicitated the
human body as incarnation of a subject;

we explicitated the subject as involved in the world through the body; we showed the world as clinging to the incarnated subject. We thus explicitated what the philosopher, in his attempt to define man, means by the term "existence."

Existence as Human Essence

This definition of man concerns itself with man's essence, with his nature, with his very being. There are, however, existential philosophers who refuse to speak of the "nature" of man. This is understandable in so far as existential philosophy is involved in a struggle against that dominant trend in philosophy in which man is presented as a mere "piece of nature." Nature is here always seen in terms of things and the existential philosopher therefore refuses to use the concept "nature" in his definition of man. He thereby expresses his refusal to place the being of man on the same line with the being of a letter opener (Sartre). To do so would result in our overlooking the *existing subjectivity* which man is. Once we understand this we no longer can object to existential philosophy on the basis of its refusal to consider the "unchanging essences" of man and things. "The essence of man (*Dasein*) lies in his existence" (Heidegger). We should note here, however, that some existentialists have developed an epistemology in which it is difficult indeed to find a place for essences, if we define an essence as "that through which something is what it is."

The Pre-reflective Existing Cogito

To say that the being of man is his being-in-the-world is to say too little. Materialism also could claim such a formulation in so far as it could define man as a particle in an infinite cosmic evolution. Nor should we see man's being-in-the-world in the same way in which we see a cigarette in a cigarette box, for this view would overlook man's subjectivity.

And without subjectivity the cigarette would remain invisible and incomprehensible in its box. The statement: "the cigarette is in the box" already presupposes a subject who can take distance from the cigarette and traverse the space to the sides of the box and back. The being of man is a *conscious* being-in-the world, a world-experiencing living being (*Welterfahrendes Leben*, Husserl). Because man's being is a being-conscious we can say with Heidegger that man is the being who in his being is concerned with his being. Man's concern for his own being defines what man *is*. Man is essentially characterized as an understanding relationship to being (*Seinsverständnis*).

It would be erroneous to conclude from this that consciousness must include a complete awareness of all that which existence encompasses as unity of mutual implication of subject and world. This certainly can never be the case. Let us suppose that I want to know how many cigarettes are left in the cigarette box. I might say "there are only six left." Thematically I am present to my cigarettes, that is, to the object of my counting. But at the same time I am present to a manner of existing in which objects can be counted; I enter into a quantitative universe. Yet, this presence to a quantitative universe is not a thematic one. My counting is "consciousness (of) counting" (Sartre), not "conscious *of* counting." It is possible, of course, to become conscious of counting. In that case I seek the specific meaning of a manner of existing which is called "counting." My approach here is one of thematically approaching the phenomenon of counting and of expressing clearly what appears to me. This "frontal attack" on the problem of counting is possible only because I already "know" what counting is since counting is consciousness (of) counting. Sartre speaks in this connection of the necessity of all reflection to be preceded by a pre-reflective "knowledge."

This is true for all modes and modalities of existence. Existing is consciousness (of) existing. Man as existing *Cogito* is a pre-reflective *Cogito*. Reflection means the return to the immediate "*irréfléchi*," that is, to living. This is possible because life is world-experiencing life (*Welterfahrendes Leben*). Our life is *human* life in so far as it is life-of-a-subject which unfolds itself while bathing in a certain light. This "light" is the existing subject himself; it is the *lumen naturale* which ultimately makes possible any insight whatsoever. Man cannot place himself outside this *light*, without losing all intelligibility. Our judgments can be true and meaningful only as long as they find their foundation in "lived experience" (*expérience vécue*, Merleau-Ponty), in the "knowledge" of man as conscious-being-in-the-world.

The Soil from Which Philosophy Springs

In the preceding section we actually found a new way of expressing the method of existential phenomenology.

Phenomenology is a philosophical method which seeks to penetrate to the indisputable roots of our thinking. As such it presupposes a return to our "lived-world," to the world of our original experience. To sever the connection with the "lived-world" means to place oneself beyond meaning. The original experience refers to the being of man as a conscious-being-in-the-world, as existing subjectivity, as "natural light" (*lumen naturale*). We must start from subjectivity (Sartre). Whatever is intended in whatever judgment we make, it is always already "known" in the light of existence. The philosopher *expresses* this "knowledge," he transposes the lived experience into concepts.

The realm of the unreflective (*l'irréfléchi*) is itself the fertile soil from which philosophy springs. A philosophical judgment is the explicitation of the pre-reflective *Cogito*. The pre-reflective *Cogito*, therefore, is the source from which all truth wells up. This emergence of truth is

a historical event. A new history of truth
starts with every new subject. The existing subject is the letting-be (*Seinlassen*) of
the world. Truth emerges in a letting-be
of the world. Man cannot remove himself
from his entanglement with the world: as
man he is determined by this relationship.

Philosophical reflection finds its own
basis in pre-reflective life. This pre-reflective life should be considered neither as
an alienation from the self nor as a preparatory stage which would end as soon
as the subject re-turns to himself in reflection. Man is *essentially* an existing
subject. The existing subject is access to
truth. No other access is possible. It is
thus possible to define existence as access
to truth, as standing-in-objectivity, as
"seeing" of reality. This "seeing"
should, of course, be interpreted in the
broadest possible meaning. "Seeing"
should refer here to the presence of a subject to any reality whatsoever. This "seeing" is the criterion of truth. The philos-

opher attempts to express in truth the deepest meaning of reality, of life. His observations and judgments are true and objective in so far as he "sees" that about which he speaks. That which is seen cannot be doubted.

Abstraction and Abstractions

The phenomenologist, trying to understand existence, refuses to make use of what he calls "abstractions." He does not deny in this the importance of abstract predicates. On the contrary, he tries to formulate the *essential* structures of existence and in this formulation he uses abstract and general predicates. The phenomenologist does not object to the abstract nature of *intelligere* but he rebels against the use of artificial, abstract concepts which have lost all real relationship with our *lived* experience. Philosophy can falsify experience and therefore can falsify reality. The real task of philosophy is to express the pre-reflective *Cogito* without distortion. When a philosophy loses touch with our original, lived experience we speak of its pronouncements as "abstractions."

The Attitude of the Subject

Once we understand the meaning of subjectivity we understand also how the appearance of our world depends in part on our own *Einstellung* (Husserl), *attitude* (Merleau-Ponty) or frame of mind. The world "clings" to the subject which man is. Yet, there is not simply one world-in-itself (*monde-en-soi*) but rather an infinite number of worlds which cling to the subject's infinite number of attitudes. What can be the meaning of this?

First of all, it is clear that our *corporality* consists of a Gestalt of numerous attitudes to which many worlds remain attached. How can there be a visible world? Part of the answer is found in the fact that I have eyes. There is a visible world attached to my eyes, and in the world attached to my ears there is nothing to be seen. My ears correlate with a

63

sonorous world. The tactile world clings to my fingertips and the mobile world to my feet. The world of handling and grasping has no meaning when I see it in relationship to my feet. My feet are "I-who-am-walking" or "I-who-can-walk." The meaning of the world is partly constituted by my corporality.

Praxis also plays its part in constituting the meaning of the world. The world of the salesman is different from that of the chemist or the politician; the world of the educator is different from that of the architect. It would be impossible to make any sense out of these many worlds without consideration of the different forms of *praxis*. We should define *praxis* in the broadest possible sense in which it will refer to any mode of existing as long as this existing is seen as a being-"at"-the-world. The preposition "at" indicates here the dynamic quality of existing which will not allow us to view the being-in-the-world of man the same way we might view the being-in-the-drawer of a pencil. To be man means to be dynamic, active. The many worlds of man cannot be understood without an understanding of *praxis*. A church tower has a different meaning for the sacristan than it has for the prankster who rings the church bells for kicks. The airplane pilot might see the tower as an obstacle to be evaded, while a tourist might use it as a point of orientation. To all these people this tower is something very different.

Thirdly, we must consider *love* as an attitude by means of which certain aspects of reality become visible. The true meaning of the other as other, i.e., the meaning of the other as subject, becomes visible only through love. An attitude of preoccupation with ourselves, with our own desires and interests, precludes our access to the true meaning of the other.

Finally, we must consider a *particular phase of history* as an *Einstellung* or attitude within which a particular reality becomes visible. A physicist must have

65

reached an advanced phase of development as a physicist if he is to understand the latest developments in nuclear theory. The Jews of the Old Testament recognized the objective immorality of polyandry but their morality had not yet reached the progressive phase of history in which the immorality of polygamy could be recognized. Jewish life at that time had not yet reached monogamy.

Many readers will object to this and remind us that with respect to the Jews of the Old Testament matrimony *was* monogamous, even though they themselves did not recognize this. Such an assertion, however, is based on a more advanced phase in the history of morality. To impute this position to the early Jews amounts to a falsification of history. Something similar happens when we maintain that a tangible world would exist even though all men would be shaped like billiard balls. While speaking of such a tangible world, we secretly attach little arms to the billiard balls. The verb *to be* has no meaning unless it refers to a subject-with-a-particular-attitude.

An Example

After this rather theoretical exposition on the concept of a subject's *Einstellung* or attitude, we might do well to give a concrete, illustrative example.

For this purpose let us inquire into the meaning of water. Ordinarily I might think of water as something that I use to bathe in or something that might quench my thirst. On a fishing trip my attitude toward water changes so that on the lake I am confronted with water that supports and hides an object of my search. The water of the lake which supports my boat is not the water that fills my bathtub or my drinking glass. Nor do I swim in fishing water. My attitude again changes when I assume the role of a firefighter; water now shows itself as a means to extinguishing a destructive fire. If I had never participated in the act of extinguishing a fire, water would never have acquired its meaning of "extinguisher of fires." Falling through the ice of a river on a cold winter day can show me the most frightful aspect of water. Nobody has ever drowned or frozen to death in H_2O. Water acquires its meaning of H_2O only within a particular attitude, an attitude in which I operate from a technical analytic point of view. Outside this attitude, the assertion that water is H_2O makes no sense. Some will maintain that the water of our bath or of our boat-trip nevertheless *is* H_2O. Such an assertion betrays that the objector has removed our attitude as bathers and tourists and has assigned to us secretly the attitude of chemists.

The Ontological Meaning of Integral Experience

Our thinking on reality has suffered deeply from a pernicious historical trend. Most of us have been taught to believe that water would admit of only one absolute and objective interpretation and this interpretation would be the scientific H_2O. The symbol H_2O allegedly referred to *real* water, to water-in-itself. This teaching is scientism and represents as such a catastrophic impoverishment of reality. Surreptitiously, the physicist is proclaimed to be the prototype of man, and his world is the only one to achieve ultimate validity. All reality is supposed to be expressed quantitatively and whatever cannot be expressed in quantitative categories is not really real. The infinitely rich *lived world*, which attaches itself to human existence with its unending variety of *attitudes*, is reduced to the poverty of a system of meanings revealed by the one attitude of the scientist. Whatever cannot be made to fit into this narrow scheme is declared to be mystification, romanticism or even a result of bad mental hygiene!

But such an approach brings up the old question of just what kind of world physics is talking about. In the lived world of the physicist there may appear "a respected and loved wife'' as an objective meaning but the physicist is unable to express that meaning as long as he confines himself simply to the terms of his trade. *As physicist* he could not even distinguish between a dead person pure and simple and a murdered person; yet there *is* a difference. Nor can he *as physicist* recount the difference between the soft red of a carpet and the sticky red of coagulated blood, between the seductive red of lips and the healthy red of a radiant young face; yet, there *is* a difference.

We might ask where it is that miracles happen and we will have to answer: ''in the religious world!'' Does the physicist as such enter that world? Is it really necessary to get a laboratory report on tears that well miraculously from a stone Madonna? Do we need a lab report to ascertain a miracle? When an engineering student travels with his fiancée to Niagara Falls he had better not limit his world of meanings to those taught him at his technical school. The Falls should mean more to him than mere "available energy" (Heidegger). Without that surplus of meaning the very idea of a vacation would be impossible, let alone one of marriage.

We must conclude that there are more than just one world. It is unacceptable to reduce everything to a world-in-itself. There are many worlds and none of these is less, nor more objective than the world of the sciences (Buytendijk). In this plurality of worlds, in this *lived world*, we find man involved with all of his many attitudes. It is here that we find the integral experience upon which all thinking is based and from which all judgments issue. "We must restore to experience its true ontological weight" (Marcel). The integral experience of which we spoke earlier constitutes the pre-scientific knowledge upon which all sciences, including philosophy, are based. The accusation that "existentialism hardly sees any continuity between pre-scientific knowledge and that which it offers as philosophical speculation'' must be counted among the many misunderstandings existentialism has endured.

A New Theory of the Sciences

We will now discuss briefly the most important implications of phenomenology for the theory of science. This discussion must first of all turn to the phenomenological theory of experience in its original meaning. Ultimately all sciences deal thematically, methodically and critically with a *specific* moment of our experience. If we define experience as the meeting of a subject-of-many-attitudes with reality, we immediately see the fallacy of Comte's scientific ideal. Every particular attitude of the subject opens a specific field of actualities. The formulation of reality, as it is guided by scientific inquiry, proceeds toward an articulation of the many different systems of meaning. These articulated systems cannot be reduced one to the other, nor can they be added together like a mosaic (Kwant).

72

Only if we define experience as a mirror reflection of a world-in-itself does it become possible to think about multiple scientific efforts as aiming at a grand synthesis from which all misunderstanding and incompatibility has been removed. However, the facts of scientific life tell another story. With the advance of the sciences the different scientific disciplines seem to have moved farther and farther apart. Often scientists of the one discipline find it impossible to communicate with scientists of the others. This fact becomes eminently comprehensible within the phenomenological framework. An actively developing scientific discipline eventually becomes aware of its own intrinsic *attitude* and stops confusing it with the *attitude* intrinsic in the other disciplines. A scientific discipline cannot start on its way to real progress so long as there subsist some basic confusion about the *attitude* peculiar to that discipline. As long as that confusion exists, a particular discipline cannot de-

73

velop because it has not yet determined the particular region of reality to which it is committed.

For example, sociology could not advance as a science so long as it held on to the scientific ideal belonging to physics. A psychological science of lived personal reality could not even start until the attitudes inherent in chemistry and mechanics had been overcome. Physics could not advance as a science as long as it remained imbued with theological points of view. Thus we see some early physicists designate the earth as the center of the universe on the basis of theological speculations concerning Christ's incarnation. The conclusion to be drawn from this is that those who pursue different disciplines *should not be expected to be able to communicate with each other* as long as they remain within the attitude peculiar to their disciplines. If in fact they do make sense to each other it is because one of them has temporarily taken over the attitude inherent in the other's dis-

cipline and lives in his world. Or else,
they unwittingly fail to understand each
other because of the plurality of meanings attached to the very same words. A
physicist and a theologian, for example,
cannot converse about "causality" as
long as this concept remains anchored in
the respective attitudes inherent in their
disciplines.

We can therefore see why none of the
sciences, in the narrow sense, can furnish
any proof concerning the existence of
God. The sciences can neither support
theism nor denounce atheism. A scientist
submerged in the attitude of his discipline could not even know what we are
asking of him when we request a proof of
God's existence. For a long time it seemed
as if the sciences gradually were eliminat-
ing God from all reality. Some might
even see this to be the task of the sciences.
Actually, the sciences consistently ex-
posed religious encroachment upon terri-
tory outside the reach of the religious
attitude. In so doing the sciences actually

purified the religious attitude. The religious realm gradually acquires a purely *religious* meaning so that it becomes impossible to extend the power control of religion over other realms of human endeavor. In the past we have witnessed many dramatic confrontations between these realms and religion. The misunderstandings and attending suffering are parts of a crisis through which man must live in order to reach new levels of insight.

The development of the sciences offers itself as a clear refutation of the idea that experience would be nothing but a mirror reflection of a world-in-itself. The more advanced scientists long ago abandoned the scientific ideal of Comte. Phenomenology shows us that we are not dealing here with a decline and breakdown of the scientific enterprise but rather that we are witnessing the coming of age of particular sciences.

We have also seen that Husserl did not develop his philosophy into an ontology of man as openness even though he described consciousness (which is a *mode* of being-human) as intentionality. Husserl started his phenomenological investigation in search for a *method* which would reach the foundation of knowledge. The phenomenological method was designed to reach the indubitable basis of thought and the *reduction* remained an essential part of this enterprise. In Heidegger phenomenology develops into a philosophy of man as openness. It is remarkable that the reduction which remains so essential a part of Husserl's *method*, seems to be absent in Heidegger. Actually, the reduction does form a part of Heidegger's philosophy; we find it there in the form of the destruction of the history of ontology. In Heidegger we find phenomenology used in a larger sense and not merely as a *method* to reach the indubitable. Phenomenology assumes in Heidegger the form of a complete philosophy, at least in so far as "complete" means anything at all in philosophy.

What we have said thus far concerning phenomenology should make it clear that as a philosophy it includes *at least* a philosophical anthropology, a cosmology, a criteriology and a philosophy of science. The habit of speaking about phenomenology as if it were a *method* is merely a carry-over from the early days in which this philosophy found its inception. It only gradually dawned on the philosophical world that a totally new philosophy had come into existence.

THE "PRIMITIVE FACT"
OF EXISTENTIAL
PHENOMENOLOGY

ture. We might say that the height and depth of understanding to which a philosophy can bring us ultimately is determined by the *"primitive fact"* of that philosophy. What do we mean by this?

The "Primitive Fact" As Unifying Principle

The meaning of the "primitive fact" was brought out by Dondeyne, who showed that every great philosophy has a central reference point, an original intuition by means of which this philosophy effects a clarification of the complexities of reality. Dondeyne showed this to be true for scholasticism as well as for the philosophies of Descartes, Kant, Hegel and Bergson. No philosophy is ever content to remain immobilized before the original complexity of the abundant and immediately given reality. Such a philosophy, if it existed, could not achieve much beyond a haphazard description; it would not be more than "a tale told by an idiot." The philosopher tries to achieve a certain unity underlying diversity; he seeks to uncover structures, his aim is to *comprehend* (Brunschvicq). The philosopher does not *start out* with a particular scheme in which he sets down how this comprehension shall be worked out. The guiding intuition of his thought is not consciously thought out first and then subsequently applied. We may not be very far amiss when we say that the philosopher has originally a hunch that a certain approach might prove fruitful. Yet, all this takes place without any conscious intellectual deliberation, without a clear understanding of what he is doing, where it may lead, from where the basic intuition derives, etc. Many times it is the patent sterility of an earlier form of thinking that furnishes the hidden impulse toward new manners of thought. Yet, the new manner of thinking often remains dark to itself while it sheds its first feeble light on the old problems of mankind.

So it may happen that a psychologist becomes suddenly aware of the sterility of physiological explanations of puberty while, at the same time, he becomes hesitantly aware of some other way of looking at the problem which promises new insights and meanings. But, during this transformation he never loses sight of the problem of puberty. He does not forget about his subject matter in order to examine the nature or the process of intuition. He suddenly sees the problem of puberty in a new light, yet, he does not then turn from the problem to examine the light in which it now appears! This light becomes only later, the express theme of research. This research is usually not undertaken by the person who "discovered" this light, or made use of it. Thus we can understand how it is possible that the philosophy developed by Husserl and Heidegger could be understood better by others than by the authors themselves.

Existence As Semidarkness

None of this should surprise us. Much of what happens in the life of man takes place in a kind of twilight. Inasmuch as he is conscious existence, man knows what he is doing; yet, in another sense he does *not* know it. He does not escape himself, but neither is he entirely transparent to himself. Philosophizing is also a part of living, and twilight and opaqueness are not strange to it. A new manner of philosophizing signals a new way of living. And there is no life, no way of living, which is not attended by opaqueness and transparency, by light and darkness. We must also remember that the first task of our thinking is to express reality; only secondarily does our thought turn upon itself in order to clarify itself. The manner in which reality is expressed comes only "after the fact" the express object of scrutiny.

A particular philosophy starts on its way as a certain movement, a certain style of thinking and it is only much later that we achieve a clear insight into what this philosophical movement really intended. At first we can only find a certain style and remain without a clearly delineated concept of the "primitive fact" through which this style *is* what it is. As far as existential phenomenological philosophy is concerned, these problems of the "primitive fact" belong to the past. The central reference point of this movement, of this style of thought became gradually clear after the existentialism of Kierkegaard and the phenomenology of Husserl merged in the thought of Heidegger. The fundamental intuition of this movement consists in the idea of existence, or the almost synonymous idea of intentionality.

Existence As Encounter, As Dialogue, As Participation, As Presence

Many authors have searched for words and concepts which would describe as clearly as possible the "primitive fact" of existential phenomenology. The *principal* purpose has been to express how impossible it is to think about a subject without thinking of his world, or to think of the world without reference to the subject. The term *encounter* probably best fulfills that purpose. Encounter is unthinkable as long as we insist on separating the two terms of the meeting. An encounter is not an encounter if a subject does not meet with "something." If the subject does not meet something, then, he does not meet at all; the "something" or "somebody" is necessary if we are to speak of meeting or encounter at all. Nor could the "something" or "somebody" function as a term of the encounter or meeting without the encountering subject. Both terms of an encounter are inseparably linked together.

There is also a serious drawback, however, to the use of "encounter" as expression of the unity of mutual implication of subject and world. In ordinary speech this word "encounter" or "meeting" usually refers to the getting together of at least two *people*, two subjects. Yet, as a recognized technical term, the word "encounter" can refer also to the meeting of man and object.

The term "dialogue" also appears particularly attractive. Existence is a dia-logue, a conversation in which both partners participate. To remove one of the partners means to remove the whole of the dialogue. Neither of the two participants in dialogue can be thought in isolation from the other without destroying the dialogue itself. The unity of subject and world is a dialetical one; it is a unity of dialogue. Here we find the primal source in which all further philosophical judgments find their origin. The dialogue cannot be reduced to simpler elements. The reductive step that tries to go beyond dialogue leads to nothing. Whoever speaks about the subject-pole is faced immediately with the object-pole and vice versa. The expression of dialogue as existence is called "dialectics."

Yet, other terms have been brought

forth to express the "primitive fact" of existential phenomenology. Marcel prefers to speak of *participation* by which he means both a "having-a-part-in" as well as a "being-a-part-of." Merleau-Ponty speaks of *presence*—as does Marcel sometimes. This term also expresses the same "primitive fact" in so far as presence cannot be thought apart from the "something" or "somebody" to which the subject can be present. Neither does presence have any meaning if we remove the subject.

This discussion so far has yet to answer the question about the height and depth of insight that can be achieved by this new philosophy. We have already concluded that the "primitive fact" of existential phenomenology can be found in the idea of existence or in the synonymous idea of intentionality. The future of this philosophy is determined by this original starting point and to evaluate that future we must question the real meaning of intentionality or existence.

How broad is the basis afforded by the concept of existence? How much can be built on this foundation? What is the "horizon" of existence, and which are its true dimensions?

Existence and the Question of God

The question concerning the existence of God and the meaning of religion are often brought to the fore in discussions about the strengths and weaknesses of existential phenomenology. Is it possible for existential phenomenology to affirm man as movement-toward-God in view of its particular "primitive fact"? Can this philosophy affirm the existence of God? The whole history of philosophy, including the recent developments of phenomenology, shows that the answer to these questions does not emerge at the end of a philosophical endeavor but is, on the contrary, given right from the start. In the very first impulse of a philosophical movement this question meets with a decision.

In Sarte, we find existentialism defined as an atheism. Yet, even without this later definition, we can find this atheism imprinted on the very first assumptions of this thinker. The "primitive fact" of Sartre's philosophy prevents the development of any religious insights. Whether or not a philosophy can have religious significance is determined at the very onset of that philosophy. Merleau-Ponty's work is similarly atheistic from the very start. Both authors are guided in their thinking by a "primitive fact" in which intentionality or existence is understood as *exclusively* a unity of mutual implication of subject and *world*.

When Merleau-Ponty defines man as *nothing but* a project of his world, *nothing but* possibility-toward-engagement in mundane situations, he already has opted for atheism. What can be the meaning of man as movement-toward-God after we have decreed that the meaning of man will be exhausted when his being-in-the-world is fully grasped, or after we have assumed that the horizon of existence is *exclusively* mundane? Under these assumptions the affirmation of God can be no more than the affirmation of an god-like absolutized mundane appearance or a degraded world-like Transcendence. The affirmation of God cannot then amount to the essential minimum it is supposed to be, viz., the affirmation of the Transcendent.

A closer reflection upon the God rejected in Sartre's philosophy will acquaint us with very strange theology. For Sartre God is in the first place the *"artisan supérieur,"* a sort of super *homo faber* who in the act of "producing" man pre-empts him of all possibility toward freedom. God is in the second place "absolute stare" (*regard absolu*) under the impact of which all men turn into objects of the world. In the third place God is the contradictory identification of "in-itself" and "for-itself." Little work or insight is required to make it clear that these definitions do not help us understand the God of religion. Certainly the God of Christian religion could not truthfully be defined this way.

On the other hand, Sartre's definition contains also much just criticism, which, although not really valid for the religious community as a whole, nevertheless applies to certain members. Actually, Sartre shows the irreligious admixtures of religious convictions. It is exceedingly difficult to think the Transcendent as truly Transcendent. The creation of the earth cannot be understood, for example, by means of similies and analogies derived from the production of objects. The idea of a first immovable mover is not subtle enough to allow for man's subjectivity. The idea of God as the "absolute stare" is preposterously inadequate. Certain religious pedagogues have influenced their followers by the use of this idea. The results of this influence are best known to psychiatrists.

93

Is a "Primitive Fact" a Dogmatic a Priori?

When we referred above to the fact that the affirmation of God cannot amount to the essential minimum it is *supposed* to be if man is conceived as enclosed within a mundane horizon, we did so rather cautiously. This caution is not groundless because the philosopher had as his task critically to evaluate what is tenable within any particular conviction. He must carefully examine the evidence, even in such a wide-spread affirmation as that of God. In this critical endeavor he is not to decide over the outcome of his research before he starts it. Both Sartre and Merleau-Ponty are victimized by their own premature *a priori* which defines existence *exclusively* as related to the mundane realm. This *a priori* decides without further ado about the most important philosophical questions. This is dogmatism!

We hope we are not misunderstood on

this point; we are not making *a priori* an uncritical plea for the inclusion of an extra-mundane realm in the subject's intentionality or existence. The question concerning the subject's orientation to God can be decided only *after* philosophical reflection. The philosopher must leave room for this reflection at the starting point of his endeavor. But to exclude such reflection through limitations in the "primitive fact" is an intolerable procedure. The "primitive fact" of a philosophy should be accepted in an attitude of faithfulness to reality. Without this, we are left with nothing but a form of dogmatism.

For us the "primitive fact" of existential phenomenology is intentionality or existence seen as openness; as openness of the subject toward that which the subject is not himself. All material objects belong in this latter category. The unity of mutual implication of subject and world is an *essential* moment of existence. But this is not to say that the openness

95

of subject toward world must be *closed off* at this point with the result that the extra-mundane is concluded. Such terms as "encounter," "dialogue," "participation," and "presence" can be maintained, however, for they possess enough flexibility *if* further reflection would force us to use them in an expanded sense.

THEMES OF EXISTENTIAL
PHENOMENOLOGY

5

Phenomenology today is no longer merely a method; it has developed into a "complete" philosophy. Once we grasp this fact, we no longer need to be surprised when we find phenomenologists of today concerning themselves with the very same great philosophical themes which have fascinated man throughout the ages.

A New Atmosphere of Thought

The idea of intentionality or of existence is entirely new in the history of philosophy, at least when this idea is considered as the "primitive fact" of thought. The phenomenological approach to old philosophical problems takes place within its own sphere; all "comparisons" with the results of other philosophical investigations therefore are somewhat pointless, especially if this "comparison" is made more or less in a material fashion. Sometimes we hear someone comment that this or that insight of phenomenology already was known to scholastic philosophers. We do not want to contradict such comments except to say that there is at least as much falsity as there is truth in such statements. Even though a phenomenologist might say the very same thing said before by other philosophers, the undeniable difference in these two utterances lies precisely in the sphere of thinking from which they spring. When those utterances are compared in a more or less material fashion, it is precisely this difference in sphere of thinking which is overlooked. This particular sphere of existential-phenomenological thinking becomes clear only after a longer exposure to this type of thought. The special sphere of a trend of thought only reveals itself upon intensive contact. As Merleau-Ponty once said, phenomenology is inaccessible except through a phenomenological method.

Besides shedding new light on old themes, phenomenology also has some themes of its own. One of these themes deserves our special interest since it proves to be of central importance for man's thinking. We have reference here to the theme of the historicity of human existence. In studying the implications of historicity, one can clearly see that phenomenology as a "complete" philosophy develops also a metaphysics, ethics and philosophical sociology. Earlier we already mentioned the phenomenological development of philosophical anthropology, cosmology, criteriology and the general theory of science.

Existence As "Already" and As "Not Yet"—Project

To see man as subjectively-involved-in-the-world leads us to the confrontation of the problem of historicity. Existence is not something "static"; the subject which man is, does not lie frozen in the facticity of body and world. His being-in-the-world is at the same time a being-toward-the-world. Being-man is a dynamism which goes by the name of history.

Let us see what the meaning of this is. We must concede that, although existence is more than a purely static reality, it nevertheless displays a static aspect. "Facticity," "particularity," "situation," the "already" of existence, all are expressions which insinuate a certain static quality when applied to the subject. When we describe a person in ordinary common language, this static quality becomes even more obvious. We might then speak of someone as "fat," "stupid," "hairbrained," "bald" or "gullible." Yet, all facticity includes a "being-able-to-be" just as every "already" opens the door on the "not-yet."

Being-able-to-be forms *one part* of the reality of facticity. On the other hand, there is no true being-able-to-be without a certain facticity. Existence, then, is a oppositional unity, a unity of contrasting factual-being and ability-to-be. Heidegger reserves the term *Entwurf* (project) for this oppositional unity. Sartre refers to the same thing when he says that man is not what he is and is what he is not. Man is not exhaustively defined in his facticity, he also *is* a being-able-to-be even though this *being* is not facticitous. Existence is a project.

In contemplating these aspects we should not lose sight of the fact that both the factual being and the being-able-to-be are forms of being *belonging to the subject*. The obesity of a fat man is not a fact in the same sense that the huge bulk of a dead elephant is a fact. A young girl *is* not pure in the same sense that a lily *is* white, and an old man *is* not bald in the same sense that a billiard ball *is* smooth. Also, the being-able-to-be of the subject differs from the being-able-to-be of an object to which "something can happen" (Heidegger). The project which man is, is a self-projecting project.

The Subject As Affirmation and As "Nihilation"

Sartre treats the intentionality of the subject descriptively in terms of "nihilation" (*néantisation*). The fact that I am conscious of this table turns out to mean for Sartre that I am conscious of *not* being identical with the table. Similarly, to become conscious of myself as a waiter means to become conscious of the fact that I am *not* identical with being a waiter. Intentionality finds in Sartre an explicitation in the direction of its negative meaning. Intentionality is pure nihilation to Sartre.

This approach by-passes all positive

with his world and can be in opposition to it. Heidegger speaks of *Heimat* (my country in which I am at home) to characterize the world as it emerges before my affective "yes." My affective "no" leads to an inhospitable world which Heidegger describes as "*unheimlich*," i.e., a country in which I am not at home. All this constitutes what man *is* as existence.

The affective affirmation of the world entails the unification of the subject. The affirmation of the self on the affective level brings about a certain fullness of being, a certain full-filment and satisfaction which we might call happiness. But the affirmation of the world never achieves complete unity; there always is a certain amount of reserve in our approach to the world. The same is true for the self-affirmation of the self on the affective level. The unity of self with self is never completely realized. All fullness of being appears together with an equiprimordial emptiness. All our experiences of fullness and satisfaction are corroded by restlessness and dissatisfaction; all peace and happiness is interpenetrated by strife and unhappiness. We have to consider all these aspects in our search for a description of what human existence *is*.

Existence As "Having to Be"

There is between subject and world an affective distance which cannot be overcome and which therefore is termed "infinite distance." The unity of subject and world is undeniable, yet the reverse, the negativity which interpenetrates this unity is equally obvious. No vigorous assertion of any worldly value escapes negation; no "yes" can remain entirely innocent of a "no." No assertion can ever achieve pure positivity, pure "yes." To be human therefore means never to be entirely finished with a task; we are never completely finished with anything. To be human means to be always unfinished. Heidegger speaks in this connection about *zu sein* and Sartre about

107

avoir à être. Both see being-man as a *having to be*. Non-being pursues us constantly; non-being penetrates the heart of being as a worm eats its way into a healthy apple (Sartre). Such terms as "nihilating rupture" (*rupture néantisante*), "nothingness of being" (*néant d'être*), "decompression of being" (*décompression d'être*), all are synonymous in so far as these express the negativity on the basis of which man is called a "having to be." Man as subject is not only a "natural light" (*lumen naturale*); he also is a "natural desire" (*desiderium naturale*).

Existence As Synthesis of Present, Past and Future: History

Man is not a mere task-in-the-world; he is equiprimordially the execution of that task. It is precisely because man cannot *wholly* affirm any facticitous meaning that he continually pushes forward. Man continually reaches beyond his facticity toward one of the many possibilities which lie enclosed in his existence as project. As soon as one of these possibilities is realized it is left behind as facticity of existence. Existence has factually acquired a new meaning, and the latter again gives rise to new possibilities. Being-able-to-be always rests on concrete facticitous being. The facticitous "incarnated" meaning is subsequently affectively negated by the subject so that it is impossible for him to remain frozen in the full positivity of a "yes." The subject is continually pushed on from one affective affirmation to another. The *being* of man is a *having to be.*

The term "movement of transcendence" is used to describe man in his being as "having to be." Man constitutes a movement which continually reaches beyond itself. Nowhere is there a facticitous meaning to be found with which man can completely coincide. Man's existence is essentially restlessness. To deny this, is to deny the essence of being-man. The insight into man as transcendence justifies our use of the term "history" to describe human existence as being-toward-the-world. Transcendence is the synthesis of present, past and future. The facticity of existence, its "already," is its past. This past is not truly "past" without the future. The present is the passing of the future into the past.

This "passing" must not be conceptualized as an objectivistic process, as a flowing without a witness to observe that flowing. It is impossible to conceptualize temporality without reference to the anticipation of the future or the holding on to the past. All this presupposes a subject. The subject's presence to the world is equiprimordially a temporal being *present*. At this moment I am involved in something that is not my own subjectivity. My presence to this object is at the same time my *present;* my present is not yet past as long as my presence lasts.

My presence-to something retains a residue of my earlier encounters together with all possibilities for a future presence to the world. No "here and now" can appear entirely by itself; there is no pure independent present. The past is equally intermingled with the present and the future. Present, past and future become incomprehensible when considered separate from one another. The temporal "ekstases" imply one another, they form a synthesis. This synthesis constitutes man's existence as temporality, as history.

Man is forever a human history. Subjectivity forever nihilates facticity on the affective level in the course of its involvement with reality. Being-man therefore is forever a "having to be"; man is essentially *desiderium naturale*. As history, man is the realization of his "having to be." There always remains an affective distance, however, between the subject and the meaning established by his history. The "having to be" constitutes the force behind the transcendent movement which man is as history. Man is essentially a "having to be" because the in-

111

volvement of the subject in reality is essentially a negating movement. History, as the realization of the "having to be," is therefore *also* the non-realization of our "having to be."

What is the real object of man's desire? Or better: what is the meaning of the desire which man *essentially* is? The accent should fall here on the word "essential" because man's natural desire is not a longing in the psychological sense. Psychology always deal with longings and wishes which can eventually be renounced if they remain unfulfilled. Man *is* himself this unfulfilled and impossible longing. "Our heart is restless until . . ." (Augustine).

The reality of this longing did not remain hidden to phenomenology. Yet, as soon as we realize that the subject both affirms *and* nihilates mundane reality, the problem arises about the reality with which man-as-subject is affectively involved. We meet with almost insurmountable obstacles in attempts to ex-

112

press this situation. At least one aspect shows itself clearly: the reality with which we ultimately are involved is *not* mundane but Transcendent.

I cannot know for sure the meaning of this latter statement. Everything remains clear so long as I think of the subject as involvement-in-the-world. But this thought becomes insufficient when I seek to express the deepest meaning of the existing subject. The clarity achieved is at the expense of a devaluation of the Transcendent and of a misjudgment of the true nature of existence. The Transcendent is not a mundane object. The affirmation of the Transcendent is *not* of the same order as the affirmation of the world. The Transcendent cannot be identified in the same manner in which we identify ants or wild flowers.

Yet, the Transcendent requires our affirmation, our "yes." To deny this would be to deny man. Without reference to the *reality* of the Transcendent we cannot describe man as he truly stands re-

113

vealed. The very *being* of man as subject is a "yes" to the Transcendent. The *reality* of the Transcendent needs to be "affirmed" (Anselm).

But how can we reflect upon this problem? First we must surrender the *a priori* notion of a mankind locked exclusively within a mundane horizon. To bring the Transcendent within view we also must disregard the gratuitous warning that phenomenology *may* not, under any circumstance, develop into a metaphysics.

History and Ethics

Earlier we used the term history to point to the realization of man's "having to be." There is a certain "having to," a certain "oughtness" operative in existence. We would be mistaken if we were to conclude that man could say "no" to this "having to be." If a man refuses to realize his potential, if he refuses to build his world, he nevertheless in that very refusal builds something, realizes some-

114

thing. A man who refuses to realize his potentials at least realizes himself as a good-for-nothing, as a lazy-bones or as a foolish person, etc. A so-called withdrawal from the world immediately opens a world in which poverty, disease and disorderliness reign free; it opens a world of illiterates, of starving babies, of catastrophies (Sartre).

The man who says "no" to the "ought" of existence nevertheless realizes himself, be it in an unseemly fashion. But why do we speak here of unseemliness? Why do we call somebody who does not care in the least about anything a "bad" person? How does ethics enter into the picture? A common answer is that a person should take others in consideration in his life, that in all his actions he should be aware of the fact that he does not live alone on this planet, etc. Such an answer is essentially correct. A philosopher might say that man is a having-to-be-tied-to-objectivity. Man's being is an ethical being. The objective

115

meaning of the other-as-subject is revealed to me as an appeal to my existence. My existence is revealed as destiny-for-the-other. My being is a having-to-be-in-the-world-for-the-other. To eliminate the other from my world is to mutilate my own existence. It is in this context that we speak of *bad* actions. Badness therefore points in the direction of the unfulfilled, of the unrealized and uncompleted. We ask ourselves now who truly can be seen as having become fully man.

A Disastrous Misconception

In the Marxist view man is about to leave behind his prehistory and then will enter into a paradise of brotherhood and peace. This will come about as soon as the means of production have been equitably dealt with. As yet no one has truly achieved the full measure of his humanity, but ultimately man shall become truly man through the evolution of collective history.

Such a naïve view completely neglects

the difference between sociological and ethical forms of coexistence. It is true, of course, that to be man means to exist, and that existence always entails coexistence. Both the object-pole and the subject-pole of our experience point in the direction of other existences; I cannot think myself in isolation. Existence therefore is characterized not as "I am in my world" but as "we are in our world."

We should realize, however, that there are numerous forms of coexistence. The "we" of a family is different from the "we" of a PTA group or of a school of thought or profession; the "we" of a pleasure-trip is different from the "we" of an anthropological expedition; the "we" of the classroom is different from the "we" of the hospital ward. It is the task of a philosophical sociology to explicitate existence as coexistence; positive sociology should describe the different manners of coexistence and should formulate laws and rules governing all the different forms of being-together.

117

The "we" of the world of production and work deserves a place of special prominence in the sociological treatment of forms of coexistence. Modern means of production exert a strong cohesive influence on society. We must look to the world of work and to the world of commercial enterprise if we hope to understand what gives solidity and substance to Western cultures. It is easier to exert influence on painting or drama production through economic means than vice versa. The means of production indubitably shape the relationships between the people involved in production. The modern economic enterprise places all people into some relationship to all other people. This fact is of importance in our consideration of all these sociological forms of coexistence which are not identical with the "we" of the world of labor and industry.

Marx felt that the universal man of the future could already be perceived in rough outline in the proletariat of today.

The proletariat represents *man*, man even in the intersubjective sense. Universal man is announced in the proletariat but this announcement is couched in negatives. Particularity, individuality, has lost all meaning for the proletarian as a result of his mistreatment by the capitalists. In the process of economic repression the proletariat has lost all identity except that of workers. The proletariat had become a pure mass of solidarity. But once the revolution shall have become a fact, work will reveal its positive meaning for the humanization of man. Solidarity-in-negativity can then develop and lead to the universal recognition of all men as men. A future worldwide community of workers then will give full reality to the definitions of true brotherhood and peace.

Earlier we asked ourselves the question whether anyone had ever realized the full measure of his humanity. Is there somebody who *truly* has become fully human? Has there ever been a person who *truly*

119

recognized his own being as a having-
to-be-in-the-world-for-the-other? Is there
anyone who has made love a full reality?
Marx answers in the negative; yet he be-
lieves that the social means of production
will eventually insert true brotherhood
in the hearts of men. It is here that Marx
makes a fatal error: there is no sociological form of coexistence which *ipso facto*
would constitute the definition of ethical
forms of coexistence. Love and hate occur
in every form of coexistence, including
that of a worldwide community of workers. Why would it be impossible for func-
tionaries in such a community to ignore
or degrade the subjectivity of others? Is
this not what Stalin did according to
Khrushchev?

"Dirty Hands"

The value of a community cannot be determined by the grandeur of its constitu-
tion, the loftiness of its Fourth of July
speeches or the magnificence of the words
engraved on its monuments. The value of

a community is determined by the value of the mutual relationships of its members (Merleau-Ponty). These relationships, in order to be valuable, require the universal recognition of all men as men. A society is inhuman to the extent that it suppresses and destroys subjectivity.

The facticity of a society is never that of a "natural order"; the necessity which reigns in a society is never of the same order as the necessity which reigns in nature. The facticity of a society is shaped by man and it will never do to tie this man-made facticity to the Will of God or Providence. Both humanity and inhumanity are brought into the world by man.

The world in which we live *does* suppress and destroy subjectivity. Fanatic intolerance, often posing as authentic religiousness or "concern for democracy," constitutes a grave assault on subjectivity. So does racial discrimination and economic injustice. An economic order in which 17% of mankind possesses

80% of all the worldly resources, is an in-human order in which two thirds of the world's population is condemned to ab-ject poverty, death and starvation. With-out exaggeration we can say that murder is a way of life in our society; it forms part of the facticity of our world

Some members of society resist this quasi-process of covert murder by having recourse to overt murder; they are seized by the strong arm of the law and as mur-derers they are put to death themselves. They have "dirty hands." But what about the rest of society, those who have not openly murdered? Can they have a completely clear conscience? Don't they too have dirty hands?

If man is seen as an isolated interiority, as a Cartesian *Cogito*, as a bit of interiority separated from the world in which he lives, we can imagine someone could have a clear conscience in a decaying world. The idea of an isolated inte-riority, however, is an illusion. Man is existence, he is involvement in the world.

In our case this involvement is with a world in which covert murder belongs to the order of the day. This can only mean that man, despite his good intentions and despite his pure principles, cannot maintain a clear conscience. We all have dirty hands. It does no good to point out that I did not make this world. I live in a facticitous order which incarnates inhumanity and immorality. All that which we gratefully accept from our culture nevertheless is tainted by guilt. Our national and international congresses, our churches, our social security, our vacation and retirement benefits, all are possible thanks to an economic situation in which 17% of the world's population possess 80% of the world's wealth. I can permit myself the writing of this booklet only because I belong to this wealthy 17%.

Is a Solution Possible?

If only it were possible for man to withdraw his hands. If only it were possible

123

for man to retire to the interiority of his conscience and to live there in the purity of his good intentions and principles. But precisely this is impossible. When we withdraw our hands in order to keep them clean we still have dirty hands. To do nothing is still to do something. To do nothing means to leave everything as it is, to leave inhumanity and injustice as it is. To do nothing means to go on silently profiting from the way things are. The dirty hands and the guilt about which we speak here is not a personal guilt; we speak here of a collective guilt for which there is no sacramental absolution. This guilt can only be atoned for in a never ending effort at humanizing the world, at making the world hospitable to all. To refuse to see this is unconscionable; in time this refusal transforms the collective guilt into a personal guilt.

Is there in our "civilized world" something large enough and strong enough to make us undertake the task of humanizing the world? Indeed there is, and we refer here to the idea of love. But first we must attain a better understanding of the authentic nature of love. Love is only truly love when it transforms the objective structures of our world in such a way that these no longer can suppress man's subjectivity. Love subsequently must be incarnated in a legal order. This latter is necessary in order to prevent man from returning to a situation in which brute force can reign supreme. The legal order constitutes a barrier with which man safeguards the boundaries of his newly conquered, newly acquired humanity; this barrier holds man back from returning to earlier forms of barbarity. But there always remains the possibility that the "civilized world" will refuse to incarnate love. The "civilized world" will in that case be overrun and destroyed. Such a holocaust not only would produce its martyrs; it also would destroy "unconscionable" people with pure principles and dirty hands.

PHENOMENOLOGY
AND THEOLOGY

A believing religious person, however, needs to reach beyond these philosophical meditations whose aim it is to explore the meaning of man and God in the light of a transcendent-movement-toward-God. It is precisely the commitment to faith which opens the possibilities for new ways of thinking about God and about man as movement-toward-God; these new ways become clear in the light of *God's speaking* of Himself and of man. Man's speaking as guided by God's speaking is called theology.

This new way of thinking presupposes a new way of being, namely a being-in-faith. Theology presupposes that man recognizes his natural desire as a movement-toward-God, as a being destined-for-God. God's word only makes sense to those who place themselves in that mode of being in which their "natural desire" will tend toward God. Theology further presupposes a "movement" of God toward subjectivity. It is in this movement that man is granted his consent, his "yes" to God in which the "desire" that he is comes into real and effective being. Only this "movement" of God to man makes it possible for man to realize the ultimate meaning of his existence which comes about in an intersubjective relationship with God. This consent to God is called "faith" or "belief"; theology as "faith seeking understanding of itself" (*fides quaerens intellectum sui ipsius*, Chenu) explicitates and conceptualizes this faith from both its objective and subjective poles.

Philosophy and Theology

Certain parallels exist between the task of the philosopher and that of the theologian. The philosopher tries to bring life within the realm of thought; in a certain sense the philosopher removes himself from immediacy, from the realm of the *irréfléchi* in order to assume a critical, methodical and reflective attitude toward it. The realm of immediacy therefore is *lived* in a different personal manner, and this manner is characterized as "reflec-tive." A philosophical attitude must lead us to *self*-discovery, to the act of seeing for *ourselves* and to doing for *ourselves*.

The task of the theologian is very simi-lar in that respect. The theologian also seeks to bring life within the realm of thought; in his case this includes super-natural life. He seeks to clarify the par-ticular mode of intersubjectivity which exists between God-as-movement-to-ward-the-subject and the subject. From there he proceeds to a clarification of the nature of the dialogue between man's world as it stands revealed in the light of God's speaking. He tries to conceptualize this life of man and God.

Theology can never complete the task which confronts it; at least not as long as we see theology in terms of the "speak-ing word" (*parole parlante*). Theological words should be approached as a "speak-ing word," for words, including theo-logical words, have meaning only as long as they are words spoken by subjects; or

132

rather, as long as these words express the subject's experience of his reality.

The fact that theology "gives expression" to faith implies that theology needs philosophy. To express faith theology needs a store of *already* available and appropriate concepts. These concepts are derived from philosophy and only gradually acquire their more purely theological meaning. The fact that theologizing is guided by God's word and God's speaking does not alter the fact. All speaking, including God's speaking, uses *human* concepts; only the use of human concepts assures that man will understand.

The failure or success of a philosophy does not depend so much on what that philosophy says, as it does on what it does not say. Often a philosophy is guided by a "primitive fact" which excludes from the start a particular reality. A philosophy goes astray when it *detotalizes* reality (Le Senne). All the great philosophies are of great importance, for all great philosophers have been able to see something of importance. Systems of thought fail to the extent that they fail to reach the full richness and complexity of "lived experience." They succeed to the extent that they arrive at an integrated and harmonious conceptualization in which full justice is done to all we implicitly "know" in our "lived experience." The best philosophy is, therefore, most suitable for the theologian who tries to explicitate what is "known" implicitly in the "lived experience" of the believer.

Often in the history of thought the human subject is looked at philosophically through concepts and categories that originally referred to things. Eventually such a philosophical approach proves inadequate; the gap between the philosophical treatment of the person and our "lived experience" of him becomes too wide to breach. Such a philosophy actually harms the theological enterprise. A language which no longer does justice to a subject's experience of the other cannot serve to express the relationship between man and God. Whoever does not observe the mutual relationship between human subjects cannot observe the subject's relationship to God. A process-like treatment of the human intersubjective realm brings about a process-like theological treatment of the relationship between the human subject and God. Such a theology becomes inadequate to the task of expressing the "lived experience" of the believer; a search often follows then for more appropriate and less rigid concepts with which to advance the labor of expression of faith. In reflecting on the relationship between philosophy and religion we can clearly see that, for example, theological morality is clearly co-determined by philosophical reflections on the nature of law.

The philosopher is rooted in the past. From this past issues both inspiration as well as a certain oppressiveness. No earlier philosophy can be entirely dismissed as pure nonsense, and the philosopher needs, therefore, to study the older systems of thought. Yet, there is no complete and overwhelmingly compelling philosophy for all the ages. The philosopher therefore cannot remain entirely preoccupied with the past; he must move on. We can build better philosophical systems only by both accepting and refusing the past. The philosopher needs to work his way through our philosophical heritage in order to eventually free himself from it. Since the best philosophies are realized in this liberating movement away from that which already has been achieved, it will be to the advantage of theologians to enhance rather than curb the freedom of thought of the philosophers. The theologian must accept the paradoxical situation of granting the greatest possible *freedom* and *autonomy* to theology's old "handmaid."

Theology and Actuality

The words used by the theologian are words directed to his fellow-men. The theologian as well as his fellow-men live in *their* own time; they are preoccupied with *their* own problems, limited by *their* own possibilities, and are longing for *their* own salvation. The theologian must know the people of his time and, consequently, he needs to know the philosophy of that time inasmuch as it is in contemporary philosophy that contemporary man stands conceptually revealed. Even in his approach to the historical dimensions of Christianity the theologian must keep in mind the particular problems, longings, tasks, and hopes of *his own* time. Only in this way can the Christian tradition shed light on contemporary problems. This tradition can only be made to speak to us in a meaningful way if we force it to speak to us as people of *our* time.

The theologian therefore must remain in close contact with the hopes and anguish of his own time; only in such contact can the Christian tradition speak to him in a meaningful way. For this reason alone modern theologians of necessity must become thoroughly acquainted with existential phenomenology. Even if we leave aside the question as to which philosophy of today might best serve theology, even if eventually we should reject a *purified* and *corrected* existential phenomenology as inadequate, we still would need this philosophy in so far as it expresses the actuality of contemporary man.

There are other reasons which should encourage the theologian of today to involve himself in existential-phenomenological thought. Theology must remain in contact not only with the past and present, but also with the future. The most secure insight into the future comes about through the most intense contact with the present. Truth is born through the revealing activity of the subject-as-natural-light. As such the birth of truth is a historical event. Great thinkers are great to the extent that they see *already* what others do not see *as yet*. These great thinkers create a new philosophy in which they incorporate these new visions; these philosophers therefore represent a particular aspect of mankind of the future.

It is understandable, therefore, that theologians should want to understand as well as possible the thought of these philosophers, because in this understanding they will achieve closeness to the world of tomorrow. The great stress on tradition in theological thinking has a decidedly dangerous aspect in so far as it can bring about an attitude from which all future truth remains invisible. A continued preoccupation with St. Bernard could blind one to the particular demands which, e.g., love makes on man in the twentieth century. It is, therefore, advisable that theologians should study Marx because this author is the first to explore with sensitivity the importance of the infra-structures for the coexistence of subjectivity. Is it purely a matter of chance that today, one hundred years after the Communist Manifesto, we have as yet no developed theology of work?

Expectations

What can the theologian expect from a purified and corrected phenomenology? Not much can be said about this as long as phenomenology is not studied with greater intensity. It is impossible to ascertain the specific value of a philosophy after a merely casual study. Yet, many theologians entertain high hopes for the possibilities of this new philosophy. These hopes are often based on an intuitive grasp of the fact that phenomenology seeks to restore to philosophy a full appreciation of the personal and human side of man's being. Phenomenology makes it possible for us to reflect upon the meaning of the subject in a manner which is unthinkable within the confines of naturalistic materialism, while at the same time protecting us from the pitfalls of spiritualistic monism. It is clear that the realm of intersubjectivity

140

also could be studied fruitfully from the perspective afforded by phenomenology. Already a good deal of work has been undertaken in these directions. These completed studies on existence as co-existence could be of great importance to theology because they can serve as a starting point for a theological formulation of the concept *church*. A phenomenology of creativity and love could form the beginning of a new theological penetration into the realities of creation and grace.

Phenomenologic-Theological Meditation

When earlier we referred to Sartre's denunciation of religion and his denial of God's existence, we emphasized the point that theologians cannot simply by-pass Sartre's arguments as if these were devoid of all merit and reality. Sartre's concept of God is not entirely idiosyncratic but, on the contrary, constitutes a reality for a great many believing Christians. Sartre sees very well that the acceptance of a concept of God as "superior craftsman" (we could add: or as first immovable mover) contradicts the concept of man as subject, as contingent freedom, as historizing being. Sartre is not talking about "nothing." Whoever wants to maintain God as the universal cause of all creation must go beyond the simple conclusion of a "Necessary Being (*Esse necessarium*) based on the contingency of all beings. If man is to be seen as "effect," the philosopher's task is to search for a category of causality which can be thought to influence real beings in such a way that freedom will be "effected." The first requirement of any thought concerning the Absolute Being must be that it maintains the further possibility of thinking about particular beings in such a way that our experience of them is not violated.

All causal categories derived from our observation of objects and as they may be found in textbooks of physics are completely unsuitable to our theological need of giving expression to the real meaning of God's influence upon man-as-subject. The theologian must search for conceptual categories that are less rigid and more appropriate to his endeavor; such categories can be found in phenomenological studies in the area of intersubjectivity. There is only one category which can be thought to affect beings in such a way that freedom ensues; this category is called love.

Love *makes* the other *be subject*. Love, when understood as active movement from subject to subject, constitutes a creative force. Love makes the other *be* as a subject, if we understand the being of the subject as a certain "fullness" of being. The loved one receives his *being-himself* as a gift from the one who loves. There is a real causality, a real active influence is at work in the loving meeting of two subjects. This loving meeting *effects* a certain fullness of being, and with this fullness comes a freedom for both

143

subjects. It can easily be seen that a phenomenology of love has greater meaning for the theodicy of creation than has a philosophy of motion.

Theology can proceed from the basis of love and in this endeavor be guided by the light of God's word. The subject which man is as the result of the divine creative love is a "natural desire to see God." This desire, however, is an impotent longing. It describes what man is in the depth of his being, but the effective realization of this being cannot be achieved by man himself. Neither is it possible for man to initiate his intersubjective relationship with God. This impotence to actualize the relationship constituting his innermost being is fallen man's original sinfulness. Only in a divinely blessed movement of man toward God, in Christ, is this impotence overcome. This movement is possible only through divine *grace;* man either can reject or accept this grace. In the affirmation of God by man the miracle of

144

man's state of grace manifests itself. In the loving movement of God to man the latter is born as subject, i.e., as a unique self which surpasses all natural self-identity. The grace of the divine movement toward man creates an augmentation and an enrichment of man; the human subject is created as loving and creative. This grace does not simply *add* to the human subject but rather penetrates into the core of his being, when it restores man to himself. This loving movement of God toward man creates a real "effect" in man's "soul," in his subjectivity, and this "effect" is there as a "quality of the soul" which is traditionally called "created grace."

The subject, however, is both a *Cogito* and a *Volo*. This is also true in a deeper sense for the subject who has been blessed in the divine encounter. His cognitive and affective "yes" achieves a depth which cannot be achieved by the subject who is not blessed by the creative divine encounter. The "yes-to-God" of this subject-as-*Cogito* in his state of grace is traditionally called his "faith," the theological virtue of faith. It is by means of faith as "supernatural light" that God becomes truly God-for-man and accessible as the holy Trinity.

The subject graced with God's encounter is not only a *Cogito* but also a *Volo*. The subject-as-*Volo*, that is, as supernatural affective "yes-to-God," is called "charity," the theological virtue of love. In love God appears as loving Presence, as "guest of the soul" (divine indwelling), as God-for-man, whose meaning for man approaches the ineffable. The loving Presence is itself a grace, it constitutes anew a loving movement of God toward man and as such forms a new creative, subject-intensifying movement in which the *Cogito* and the *Volo* of the subject acquire a depth which defies all understanding. Even the most eloquent mystics are defeated in the face of this astounding mystery.

Supernatural life should truly be seen

146

as a dialogue of persons, as intersubjective communion, as progressively deepened intimacy. Yet, despite this intimacy, God remains a distant God for man. God manifests himself as loving Presence but His love fills man with an ever increasing longing for Him. The supernatural desire which man is in his state of grace cannot be satisfied on earth. Only his faith in love makes it possible for supernatural man to continue to live and not to surrender to despair. This faith in love is called "hope," the theological virtue of hope.

CONCLUSION

We have not said a word as yet to justify the title of this little book: *Phenomenology and Humanism*. Not without reason did we do this.

We Should Take Subjectivity As Our Point of Departure (Sartre)

No philosophy can justly be called a humanism if it does not do justice to the full reality of human subjectivity. Indeed we should take subjectivity as our point of departure! Yet, we should also realize that once we take that decision we have in actuality decided *nothing* as yet. The ultimate form that our humanism will assume depends in fact on the manner in which we choose to think about the subject. It also should be evident that a philosophy cannot be called a humanism on the basis of its divergence from or its coinciding with a particular *a priori* criterion of human subjectivity. To do so would amount to dogmatism. The integral meaning of the subject cannot be dictated by any philosopher, Sartre included.

Sartre writes that man must find his way back to himself through the realization that nothing can save him from himself, not even a valid proof of God's existence. On the one hand, this pronouncement indicates clearly the direction in which a humanistic philosophy must develop. Man must find his way back to himself. On the other hand, we cannot accept the *a priori* exclusion of the possibility that the subject, who has found himself, might at the same time find his way to God. Phenomenology can only escape dogmatism as long as it is made to express the *full* reality of the subject, without any *a priori* exclusions. If this expression of the full subjective reality makes it necessary for us to recognize the existence of God, we need not assume that therefore man must live deprived of his innermost nature which henceforth belongs to the Transcendent; nor need this conclusion deprive man of the authorship of his thoughts and deeds. In his "yes-to-God" man can find his way to himself as integral man. An integral phenomenology recognizes this aspect and we call it therefore a humanism.

What Phenomenology Is Not

The short discussions up to this point should make it clear that many of the once current definitions of phenomenology are no longer valid. Phenomenology is not a form of Platonism, nor is it a revived form of Aristotelian realism.

Nor is phenomenology a late edition of idealism or of irrationalism or a philosophy based by necessity on atheism. Phenomenology is not another name for introspection and it is not simply a method used in metaphysics. It is not a preparatory science which is supposed to ready us for the real work of philosophy.

Existential phenomenology is a philosophy which uses the idea of existence as its "primitive fact." This philosophy gives expression to the nature of man seen as openness-to.

It should be clear to the reader that we do not wish to recommend phenomenology as the "ultimate" philosophy. Ultimate, final philosophies will not be found so long as authentic philosophers can be found. That which persists through the multitude of philosophical endeavors is the never ceasing attempt to give full expression to the ultimate meanings of life as lived by man, to approach these meanings with ever increasing clarity, and to penetrate them with the aid of

154

ever more appropriate concepts. All philosophers have "seen" something, all philosophies deal with something.

Authentic philosophizing requires of us that we creatively approach the age-old problems of man and shape their new dimensions against the horizon of our own future. The coming generations doubtless can count on their own geniuses who will think the old philosophical problems anew through the perspective afforded by a new "primitive fact." Phenomenology will not then be reduced to meaninglessness, it shall have served its function in the history of human thought. Phenomenology will then be surpassed and the authentic philosophers will no longer feel the need to give expression to reality with the help of phenomenological categories. They will have discovered other categories.